SINGING TO

~Voices Dow ...e Ages~

BARBARA ROBINSON

dorcas imprints

First Edition: Singing To The Four Winds

First published in Great Britain in 2012 by:
dorcas imprints
132 Hinckley Road
Stoney Stanton
Leics
LE9 4LN
www.indigodreams.co.uk

Barbara Robinson has asserted her right under the Copyright, Designs and Patents Act 1988 to be identified as the author of this work.
©2012 Barbara Robinson

ISBN 978-1-907401-95-4

dorcas imprints is an imprint of Indigo Dreams Publishing Ltd

British Library Cataloguing in Publication Data. A CIP record for this book can be obtained from the British Library.

This book is sold subject to the condition that it shall not, by way of trade or otherwise, be lent, re-sold, hired out, or otherwise circulated without the author's and publisher's prior consent in any form of binding or cover other than that in which it is published and without a similar condition including this condition being imposed on the subsequent purchaser.

Designed and typeset in Times New Roman by dorcas imprints

Printed and bound in Great Britain by: Imprint Academic, Exeter

Over the years a number of the poems in this book have been included in various publications including Reach Poetry, Dawntreader, Salopeot, Dial 174, E. Tips, Carillon, Metverse Muse, Rubies in the Darkness, Aspire, Free Xpressions, Pennine Poetry, Countryside Tales, and many Anthologies.

I extend heartfelt thanks and acknowledgements to all the editors of these publications, especially Ronnie Goodyer and Dawn Bauling for their long-time encouragement and also subsequent tireless support in making this book possible. I give thanks to Tina and Lisa for putting up with my numerous questions and cries for help at Boston Spa Library and also to Bernard and David for their guidance over time.

By the same Author: *One Moment In Time*

CONTENTS

FOREWORD

This collection of poems reflects the voices of my ancestors who, in the mid 19th century, made the great trek across Russia and Europe. They eventually settled in Germany before my maternal Great Grandparents eloped to England in 1883; our beloved Granddad being born in Northumberland in 1884. Many of the old beliefs were handed down, I having inherited their great love of Nature, mythology, history and old family traditions.

Now retired I started my working life in the Accounting/Pensions sector before a second career of Occupational Therapy and Caring in the community. I have had an interest in writing since my schooldays, and although my first success was the Wetherby prize in 1985, I didn't start writing again until 2004 and that work being poetry and stories for children. My main motivation came when I subscribed to various small press poetry magazines and read their excellent poetry, gaining knowledge from the active support of the members of these worthy periodicals. I have been fortunate in finding settlement, as a writer, within an ever widening circle of literary friends and like-minded associates.

SINGING TO THE FOUR WINDS

~Voices Down The Ages~

Wishes...

mine's not for gain
of gold nor treasures,
I hanker not for fame…
I'm guided by sweet Nature's measures
that guard me, call my name.

It's of the four winds
that I sing, Heaven's
firm cornerstones,
- forever guarded by
their Angels' wings,
wherever I make my home

SONG FOR MY UNBORN SON

I scattered love in the forest
and over our home's grassy plain,
amongst the flowers, within the stream,
to be nourished by sun and by rain.

I sang our poems to the hilltops,
on sunrise pink tipped peaks
and when the four winds softly blow
our history they'll proudly speak.

I shared the stars with the Barn Owl,
the moon with all birds of the night
that they may sing many songs of hope
to guide us towards the light.

I prayed to the supreme sky God,
in his safe footsteps we might tread.
May Angels always be present
to guard us from dangers ahead.

WAITING

My troubled mind cries for the known
familiar pictures imprinted upon my soul.
Visions in a kaleidoscope - a river
meandering through a lush green vale
whilst high above, the grassy Steppes and
poppies singing colourful songs to heaven.
Father laughing as he hugged me;
Mother smiling, singing whilst she toiled,
her joyous words gloriously uplifting.

We were taught to run, long, unseen,
to climb the steep eagle slopes,
swim the ice cold waters
submerged beyond hypothermia.
All children learned the long sticks,
hands, feet, any defence.
Mother said it was for our own good.

Four kids ready for what life serves up.
Chameleons camouflaged in forest gear,
as elusive as butterflies, swifter than the
swallows climbing dawn skies,
soaring through valleys
leading back to the beginning.
Mother knew everything, was wise.

Soon worry lines etched her brow;
darkened moods marred her prettiness.
I touched the fear clouding her soft voice.
'This is still the land of the Barbarian,
go swiftly - it has to be - we will soon follow.
Today is the start of our new forever
may a beautiful sunrise await us there.'

But the kaleidoscope so cruelly lies for
my forever embraces only fearsome spectres
and my heart's grown weary of long waiting

for those kinfolk who did not follow.
Did Charon's boat glide through their darkest hour,
oars silent amid an irrevocable midnight passage
with no fleeting glimpse of a reflection
of who was left to pay the Ferryman?

We fear the Hordes swooped like a black cloud,
stole your last days and we not there to hold you.
If our Land holds no imprint of our essence,
no signature cut in earth, stone or clay
then we must come home, pray to the four winds,
sing a song to the spirits from the high places
and they will hear us, know that we have come.
No enemy will paint our history out.

EXILE

There is nothing behind
and there's nothing in front
and our past is buried
and our future's unborn;
the clouds cry their grey tears
with no sign of the dawn.

And the river is deep
and the river flows fast
and the track is crooked
hiding sight of the way
and mist has descended
veiling each gloomy day.

And the woods are so dark
with trees closely gathered
and the birds are silent
giving nothing away
and no light from the sun
pointing out the true way.

So no shadow back cast
and still nothing in front
and we now pale spectres
with our future unknown
and breeze moans it's sorrow
for the seeds still unsown.

And the mountains are cold
and the mountains are bleak
and the pass overhangs
so there's nothing but ice;
our lives still a gamble
like the roll of the dice.

And down on lone flatlands
there's nothing in front
and the river is deep
and the river flows fast,
still no future certain
that will flourish and last.

BUTTERFLY

Shy
beauty,
dazzling with
vibrant colours
and fine flittering, ballerina, dance.
Bring once again those golden days of love,
repair my heart,
teach my soul
to soar,
- fly.

SUNSET

As balmy summer air enwraps
warm arms around the tired day
kaleidoscope of colour maps
the heaven's blessed milky way.

Sky turned to sweet pink blushing rose
as would a new bride still love-shy;
warm innocence of dusk in pose,
sun's dying rays paint arc of sky.

Soon ardent fiery fancy roused,
feverish indigo, purple, mauve,
glorious hues so briefly housed
across the fading light to pause.

How soon bold colour sadly seeps
as blackbird's song ceases to trill,
edge of evening gracefully creeps
with sedate dance and all is still.

Then swift black wings of darkest night
with no whisper or no warning
erase the once bright glowing light,
beauteous breath of old day scorning.

FIRSTBORN

Barefoot child
of hill and plain,
running like the deer,
flying on wings
of innocence.

Nature's child,
poems plaited
in ebony hair,
fables written
in laughing eyes.

Precious child.
River pearl,
mountain eagle,
forest tiger.
Born to lead.

The four winds
sing his name.

EAGLE OWL

Gnarled grey branch your temporary perch,
your haunt the darksome woods and field;
you hear all secrets of the night
that neither leaf nor grass can shield.

Long tufted ears and sharpened beak,
feather soft, garbed brown and white,
you are lord of all you survey,
eyes piercing enigmatic night.

Swooping low, sharp claws uncurled,
you grasp your prey without a prayer.
So little life you've lived young vole,
and you, small mouse in flora's layer.

Learned predator fly on high,
comb the night, your vigil keep.
Till offspring sated, you must fly
where silence stirs from sleep.

SINGING IN THE DARKNESS

We're wanderers crossing life's desert,
thirsting for improbable dreams.
Such a long and perilous journey
with those hardships that fate often deals…

when the hunting is lost in deep snow;
no meat and the hunger is gnawing.
When the rivers are frozen with ice
and the dawn shows no sign of thawing.

Those delays with broken down wagons;
Nature's forces wild, multiplying.
Attacked by wild strangers at night time;
those days when our kinfolk lay dying.

But life's scales weigh good against bad,
glorious times when newborn are thriving.
The joys of the Spring and the flowers;
love, laughter and faith still surviving.

We know that when life knocks us down
we will stand tall and focus on winning,
won't show any small weakness or fears.
In the darkness our hearts will keep singing.

A GUIDING HAND

Patience inured within his veins
Father deftly taught me the ins and outs,
the making, stringing, of a sturdy bow,
the fashioning of arrows, javelin pointed
- our hunger teetered upon these skills.

Small legs wearied by the hunt
I rested on Father's sled,
- fleet footed deer sturdier than I.
But Father knew the alchemy;
quietly allowed me growing time.

He taught me to fish in icy stream,
know each fin, contour, coloured scale.
Childish enthusiasm awakened;
dipping, flashing, in psyche's depth,
lit by the love upon his face.

He showed me the high crags,
birthplace of his proud falcon.
One day I'll climb that ridge,
see my bird alight, speak his name;
be called Falcon Lord like my Father.

AND MOTHER DANCED

Her face soft, wreathed in happiness,
twirling then swirling and dancing,
reliving those times of her youth
when days were carefree, romancing.

Each step was a statement of love
for my Father, her eyes now glittering
and she waltzed in his arms as she laughed,
flirting and flouncing, skirts skittering.

Like a butterfly's wings she dazzled,
fluttering as the wings of a dove;
her pretty face turned up to the sun,
rainbow colours reflecting her love.

Warm arms enveloped us children;
flowers blossoming amid the sorrows,
making all those bad days seem better,
endowing courage to face our tomorrows.

THE HORSE SALES

I sat on the old fence, watching,
awaiting more unfolding tales,
learning the ropes for the horse sales,
wrathful whinnies, flickering tails.

Father was best of horse traders,
his name so well known on the Plains.
His mounts owned spirits of raiders,
all knew not to doubt his bold claims.

He spoke secret words to tame them
with warm words that came from the heart,
they followed him as their leader,
directions obeyed from the start.

And oh may I follow his lead now,
own that magic that's born of the soul,
learn the knowledge of our ancestors,
feel the breath of each newborn foal.

WRESTLING OLYMPIAN DREAMS

In earlier days we were ragged,
novices all bruised and joints torn.
Young bones tired, weary with trying,
our spirit quite weak and forlorn.
Then Baku said show the cold face,
be fierce, put some heart in the fight.
Go swoop like the fierce Eagle Owl,
be cunning - like he hunts at night.

We played and trained and we flourished,
we swam and we ran, felt the pain
but our pride never let us give in,
when we fell we stood up straight again.
An air of immortality reigned
like our Forefathers had known before.
It was all about honouring our name,
still renowned on each distant shore.

And Baku revealed all his secrets,
he taught us the tricks that he knew…
deftness, surprise, feint and eye stare,
oh how soon our confidence grew.
We are talking of Olympian dreams
when to win is to be only the best,
head high, show we are the champions,
that we're better than all of the rest.

FLIGHT OF THE FALCON

Claws gripping glove a wild world is
reflected in his un-hooded eyes
then with one swift glorious motion
he's flung high to ragged Autumn skies.
Enjoying flight of allotted freedom
he flies in random patterns, explores,
catches the edge of the cooling breeze
then ascending to the heavens soars
in ever increasing circles there
above the flock of oblivious sheep
before flapping wings in uncertain light
as hunger tempts him to swoop then sweep
back to the Falconer's glove and alight,
receive his reward before fall of night.

LOSS

Withdrawn into the
secret attic of her mind
her world would seem
to serenely spin,
hidden familiar spaces
filled with who knows what.
But therein lies her refuge,
warm closet of calm
and safety, a haven
from this tortuous world
where nothing owns true shape
or realistic form.
Reason to her
still an inscrutable word.

A rare smile flickers
lighting her freckled face
before flitting quickly
as in a flimsy dream,
replaced by blankness
in blue distanced eyes.
Locked out from her other
fathomless world
I suffer once more
that deep helpless ache
of loving her deeply
but no response evoked;
of holding her close
but not reaching my child.

MOVING ON

In the darkness,
in the cloak of darkness,
soft breeze speaks my name,
sings tomorrow's song
as a night jay's offering.
Although you are gone
I feel your presence
as soft whispers of love
lighting night's air.

Here in the darkness,
in the cloak of darkness,
you warm the night
and refresh the dawn…
allow me to see
a new day's choices.
You remind me to stop
and smell the flowers.

THERE COMES A TIME

"There comes a time, a moment,
when life must find a purpose.
Grow wings and flourish,
blossom as the rose and
keep steadfast as the trees.
Know the true meaning of life."

Circled in the shade
the hushed children listen,
studied faces rapt with awe.

The Scholar turns the key,
opens up fair realms
beyond their narrow sunrise;
stretches their minds
to far corners of the universe;
shows them what could be,
might be, in other Lands,
- Their imagination soon sipping
the nectar of dreams,

The Scholar's teaching
them languages this year.
Thanks, Danke, Gratae.
It's all Greek to us,
their Grandmothers.

TRANSIENCE

The withered sigh of a fallen rose
brings redolent sad air of stolen days,
a mournful dirge of summer's dying pose
as nature now frolics through Autumn's phase.
She caresses fair growth, colours some leaf,
quietly paints new scenes whilst cooling the morn.
Night and day she sneaks as a furtive thief,
her bright paint box world transforming the dawn.
Soon her grandeur changes, feels tired and jaded,
tetchy frost stings earth, late Autumn is tamed.
Withered sigh of a fallen rose soon faded,
bitten by cold aching teeth, freeze-framed.
Caressed by cold of icy proportions,
fine delicate shades now pale distortions.

WINTER FEAST

Hunger stalks these bitter wintry days
as cold wind blows, snow deeply lays.
Birds with hope, purity of grace,
through snowy branches weave and lace;
patient, awaiting benefaction
of morsels for their satisfaction.

Now silence kept though feathers flail,
swift flash of eye and flitch of tail.
I spread the feast, a lordly table,
scatter grain and rind of bacon,
a veritable feast of nuts and seed.
Come brethren from afar to feed.

A twittering armada of winged sail
swoops down to hungrily regale.
A treasured sight for my sore eyes
as Nature's art before me lies,
a token of winter sent to cheer,
I'd not be anywhere but here.

ROSE KISSED DAYS

Oh glorious seasons how swiftly you pass;
the carefree child now withered and frail.
Where are gone those days, those rose kissed days,
where dreams would rise and hopes would sail?

Where every dawn was a dew drop morning
and no hurdles were ever too high to climb;
where young bones felt urgent flush of youth,
our hopes and dreams so unknowing, sublime.

Where life would sing from a canopied tree,
with rope swing dare and deep river tease.
Wild game to be hunted, we'd run many a mile
until north star blinked on the edge of the breeze.

Oh how we lived those glorious moments;
we laughed at danger, all fear soon stilled
and whatever will come, will come, will come,
I hold memories warmed, with love fulfilled.

NIGHT SHIFT (Crimea 1855)

Rain lashes the murky streets;
a deluge of giddy raindrops
making lamplight appear to
stutter, flicker nervously.
My footsteps clatter staccato
across ancient cobblestones
drumming pitter-patter echoes.

My working world now left behind,
pain, suffering once more put aside,
concealed within a sympathetic place.
Cloaked now the stink of death and
detritus that tightly clasped my heart.
I empathise and quietly mourn
all closeness sadly torn apart.

Holding the hand of sickness
every single working moment
I have my nightmares too
when darkest dreams explode
and I find it hard to breathe;
urged to jump into the abyss,
avoid the struggle of lamp lit hours.

It's not the night time that I fear
just the stark, dark suffering,
the worn down wick of candle's flame
spluttering in the darkness,
phuttering on to an inevitable end;
when the soft voice grasps my heart;
'Please tell her I really tried'..

I've wept for all the brave souls,
mourned for what is only
a measured time of our existence.
Sighing, my footsteps quicken
towards a hopeful kindlier dawn
when sunrise might lighten my day,
let me understand life's game plan.

PROMISES - A LOVE SONG

If you see no Angels
then I will sculpt them for you.
If you see no sun
I will shine a light for you

- and if you see no heaven
I will take you in my arms,
kiss you, awaken your soul.
We'll drift into forever,
beyond the triumph of stars
where Paradise awaits.

The passing of a thousand Springs
cannot compare to my love.
As the lotus flower blossoms,
petals turned towards the sun,
so you will flourish

- wrapped within my arms,
discovering the joy
of each newborn day.
A triumph of hearts entwined;
both souls reborn.

VIENNA

Father called it
his 'Heavenly City',
its music woven
from Angel's breath
played on ocean waves
kissing golden sands.

And as the tides flow,
so we must wander,
onwards, forwards,
always chasing a dream.
Like a capricious breeze,
exploring the ins and outs,
the nooks and crannies, of life;
searching for our chosen
place in the wilderness.

Grandma once said that if
we looked beyond the clouds
we would see the sun,
feel it's warmth,
know when we were home.

A NEW DAWN

These homely rooms have stilled their song
though memories visit in the night.
His past essence, a living flame
still flickers in fire's dimming light.
I long to hear him call my name.

No rafters moan nor spirits weep,
though soon I'll say my last goodbye.
Do you see me love or hear me?
Will these walls around me let love die
or keep secure fond history.

Though footsteps rest, resound no more,
life's corridors mute in sun kissed dawn,
through open window blackbirds call
whilst poppies smile in golden corn.
Sweet glimpse of heaven's Godlier halls?

The hardest part is to close the door;
no looking back whilst I walk away.
Through my tears do I hear his soft footfall,
feel steadying arm, his warm voice say,
'I'll be there love whenever you call.'

NIGHT MAIL

Miss you,
now dimmed the light that shone.
That exquisite spark about you
blown out, and now there's none.
Lost, the song within my soul,
where has your spirit gone?
Love you,
but I've no rock to lean upon.

Miss you.
Tell me where do I step next.
I feel just like a blind man
who cannot read the text,
my lonely heart sick with grief,
my future dulled with pain.
Love you,
but I'm like a rainbow without rain.

Miss you
my Angel in the sky.
Love you lots.
P.S. Still trying not to cry.

FLYING ON WINGS OF FAITH

Many's the road now long travelled,
we've crossed wild river and plain.
Strange lands traversed and lived in;
timeless years of troubles, of pain.

It's been hard tending the wagons
and keeping the livestock alive.
We've lived many a winter in one place,
snow blizzards so hard to survive.

Though we've lost some precious kinfolk
we've been blessed at times with new life.
Sweet Nature's regeneration
to surmount the grief and the strife.

Sometimes I wish I was back home,
where the eagle flies high on the breeze,
but I hear winds speak age old wisdom
through leaves of the old forest trees.

And they're telling us we must go on,
No time for the old aspirations.
We must fly on the wings of the Fates
with strong faith and new found elation.

COMING HOME

The frothy ebb tide softly weeps
over sea shells, pebbles and sand,
spread-eagling seaweed in its wake,
deft touch of sweet nature's hand.
I become aware of my life's flow,
turmoil and stress, love and light.
A ripple on the waves for each
little hindrance or exquisite delight.

Gone chattering tongues of townsfolk throng,
quiet now the quibbling of gannet's song
until our ship breaks the peace around
with grating hoots, and raucous sound.
And I look at my girl and my unborn son
and I swell with pride and love unsung
then I gather them in with arms open wide
as we leave the dock on the evening tide.

Our new country awaits across the North Sea
and they call it England and it beckons me.
Some rivers run free and some rivers run fast,
the tracks meander, great history of past.
I hear eagle calls where the wind flows free,
there's ice on high mountains, sun on the sea.
And this now my home, ideals of the past;
and I sense our future will flourish and last.

A STIRRING IN THE AIR

I see you fraudulent morning
wearing exaggerated smile of
sunlight on late Winter's face.
Fist unclenched, cold air's
stiff fingers have painted
nature's gifts with hoary rime,
let seeping cold pervade the soil,
frosted leaves with patterned ice.

Though funeral season lingers
I feel a stirring in the air;
earth's growth quietly resurging.
A single snowdrop poses prettily,
guarded by an old stone wall.
Oh Winter come lift your veil, grant
golden Daffodils leave to ring;
the liberty to sing their chosen song.

Let us celebrate the April flowers.
Hail *Ludi Florales*.

*# Ludi Florales - a Roman, April festival in
honour of Flora, Goddess of flowers and Spring*

THE BLUEBELL WOOD

I feel the warm kiss of sunbeams
through each branch of oak and elm
as I stroll through a sea of bluebells
whose blossoms now overwhelm
my senses like the touch of Morpheus,
tempting me to keep
my silence by the crystal stream,
to lay my head and sleep.

Bluer than the summer skies,
more vibrant than the sweetest rose,
bluebells ring their beauty now,
woken from their deep repose.
A scene which makes me draw sharp breath
and hold it in deep awe
whilst drinking in this beauteous sight,
I never should crave more.

But times like this I deeply wish
that Spring could follow Spring,
more days I'd walk the bluebell path
and how my heart would sing.
I feast my eyes upon this fair,
enchanting artist's scene
and wish to hold it's hand forever,
my fragrant Elysian dream.

SLIDING DOWN RAINBOWS!

"Everything has it's place
in the order of this world.
Four winds - Angels guarding
the corners of the universe.
The sun, moon and stars
lighting up the skies;
planets in their glory
obeying the High One
-all circling in their orbits,
guided by his heavenly hand."

Father looked thoughtful,
his gaze long resting skywards.

The children sat quietly
waiting for release,
- now smirking,
small elbows nudging, knowingly,
before a soft whispering.
- ' *He's gone sliding down
rainbows again!*'

HONEYGHAN

A feline form in grass nearby
slinks past rose and hollyhock.
Soft brown feathers
from cruel jaws fly;
small furry assassin of green slant eye.
- And a sadness invades my heart.

For lying prone without a breath,
-a tiny bird with broken wing,
a beaten soul who'll no more fly
as mother wren mourns death's sad sting.
- And pain reflects within her eye.

She sings a song, a haunting tune,
each note a tear, a sigh of grief,
an iceberg's touch,
a fallen leaf,
a lonely soul without a brief.
- The lament of a broken heart.

Now furry paws tread soft on path,
a graceful form with tail held high,
a triumphant gleam in golden eye
whilst I, at loss, stand sadly by,
So helpless in death's aftermath.

OH SILENT NIGHT

Oh silent night, no sleigh bells ring,
ice crystals blink on snowy track;
frosted ferns lick the window panes
and there on sill to guide you back

A Christmas candle, long flickered out.
I close the curtains on the night,
Winter's cold face not welcome here,
not welcome where love once burned bright.

What I would give for one more kiss
to bring some warmth to pallid skin,
to feel once more the dew of love,
reap passion from this heart within.

But depicted in old photograph
on mantle shelf, above hearth's flame,
hands touching hands, assuring love,
there in Love's name you're home again.

BEVERLEY MINSTER

In awe I walk quietly down the aisle
lest my footsteps roughly tread
these ancient stones of worship;
echo around the vaulted hall
disturbing the hallowed air.

Afraid to stir St John's remains
entombed below an inscribed tablet
I gently seat myself, head bowed,
forming silent words within a prayer.
I sense the air acquiesce my thoughts;
await the feel of some angelic touch
of approval to surround my mind.

My eyes roam to the sacred altar
where Athelstan's dagger rested
until his northern battle was won.
There beside the altar,
long unused and set cold in stone,
is the Sanctuary chair…
blessed saviour of wrongful doers.

Now choir's angelic voices
dust the stone musicians
carved around the nave's walls
before rising to enwrap the
magnificent columns which soar
up as if stretching, reaching,
for Heaven's universe of stars.
I'm transported to a higher place.

At peace I listen to the message
of that other world beyond this one,
where trust and love abound.
Love and light surround me and
a special warmth enfolds my bones,
as the choir sings the final line….
'All things come to those who believe.'

ONE MOMENT IN TIME

Dreamlike glides the swan this tranquil hour
On stream of thoughts where willows softly weep,
Stirs ripples of past memories on the water,
Shares hopes with only naiads in the deep.
With uncoiled neck now reaching for the breeze
He raises graceful wings and moments soon
He's lost beyond the forest's autumn crowns,
His image just a shadow across the moon.

CHEMISTRY CLASS

Mr. Davies rarely wandered
from his sturdy desk
as if afraid to lose
the security of its solidness,
so he never caught me out.

An accident prone child
I was scared of Bunsen burners,
Catalytic chemicals and such;
afraid of blowing up my school,
so sometimes sat on floorboards,
back to bench, wrote a poem.

Couldn't find a rhyme
for Petri dish…tish…lish
so did my own thing, mind wandering
towards skies, quasars, red stars
and the mystery of Comets;
gaseous trains whirling,
swirling like a dragon's tail.
Wrote about the universe.

In my second term Mr Davies retired.
My secret world was swallowed
by a big black hole.

TRACKING

It was my turn to be the bait,
to race away and lose the pack;
leave a trail of twiggy arrows,
message small piles of leaves.

When I raced down the worn track
I hadn't meant to see the world
through overgrown hawthorn,
brambles, and broom so blown
it was taller than me.

But I was a tenacious child,
fought my way through
a screen of twigs, thorns, leaves.
The intrepid explorer
but now the hunted.

Crouched low off track
on hands and knees I stopped
now staring...eye to eye with nature.
Stoat and child, child and stoat
both mesmerized and wary,
his black tipped tail, soft fur,
enwrapping thoughts of wonder.

I was snared within his eyes....
until the hunters' cries rang out
much clearer now....tracking, trailing.
Stalemate no longer an option
I blinked then slowly retreated
bowing to majesty rarely seen.

ALWAYS SUNSHINE

Warm sunbeams glanced through leafy trees
and lit my face as I daydreamed.
In clovered grass, face to the sky,
like yesteryear or so it seemed.
For memories now were days of old
when dancing around each copse and dell,
I picked wild rose, made daisy chains,
roamed glade where sprite and bluebells dwell.

By gurgling stream I spent sweet time,
once more I was that carefree lass,
barefoot, content, toes dangling in
the shimmering waters of my past
reminding me of young life's role
then memory stole to sunlit seas,
I ran and played on golden sands,
hair tossed and blown by salty breeze.

Now sledging down high hill to vale
in rutted snow to shouts of glee,
the kiss of sunbeams on my face,
pure happiness embracing me.
In all the seasons of the year
it's strange the tricks my memory plays
for all was bright when I was young,
my childhood held no rainy days.

VISITATION
(The Shambles, York, 1586.)

A familiarity of crooked dwellings lean,
reaching out, as if to grasp some comfort
from their neighbours in these hard times.
Sensing my presence the call of livestock
echoes from behind the shops
splitting the evening's calm.
I, Margaret Clitherow, lived here…
Flesshamel, Shamel, Shambles,
street of many butchers.

Moonlight appears to dance, nervously glance
as my footsteps soundlessly drift
along these ancient cobblestones;
skulking shadows darkening door
and passageway, embracing the open gutter.
The scented cloth held to a nose
barely dispels the dreadful smell,
the hell of putrefying matter thrown
from upper windows, cast from butcher shops.

Did those who tried to diminish my faith
tell you I sheltered travelling priests,
held Mass for local Catholics at No.36.
Inspectors watching, counting, searching:
three windows on the outside
two only on the inside; they'd sometimes
find the churchmen's hiding place.
Many were their warnings and
detention in cold, dank dungeons
where I longed for many a loving sunlit dawn.

Returning home to my dear husband John
I never swerved to avoid the dark times;
no cobwebs of doubt around my doorway
enticing me to succumb to religious blindness.
I had my own truth and the Lord's love.
When the mean sharp corners of my life
scratched at my reserve I turned the other cheek.
Please do not fault that frightened child
who spoke against me, caused my final downfall;
intolerance another word the bigots taught her.

Defending my right to choice of faith
I denied my detractors the falseness of trial.
Ouse Bridge prison then my deathly abode
where I'd sewn the white shroud in which I lay
face down on cold dank flags, restrained;
upon my waistline a large stone was placed.
A door they laid upon my defenceless form,
I would not weep but quietly prayed
then stone piled on stone un-gently added
until breath departed from my tortured frame.

BARKING MAD

Great Aunt Maud liked to show her Goth side;
loved all colours as long as they were black,
her slender frame silk ebony draped
whilst thick mascara clung to eyelashes
like the soot that clasps our chimney back.
She'd loudly decreed there was no mystery
in bright garish colours, no finesse,
each shade yelling your secrets to the world.
So still boxed on a wardrobe shelf, unworn,
are red shoes; mad 'spur of the moment' purchase
meant to brighten her black linen dress.

But she must have seen the light for she'd
erased the stately plumed black horses;
deleted the dark laying out clothes.
Said she'd like to fly with the Angels
not be sick on 'him down there's boat'
so she'll wear the white dress, it's more apt.
And she's excited about flying in space.
Hates sadness so her new head square,
the one embroidered with butterflies,
must drape her white wooden coffin.
She said nobody in their right mind
would dare show sorrow to a butterfly.

Granddad reckoned she was barking mad;
had been howling to the moon one last time.

THE SPIRIT OF SILENCE

I search the skies where silence hides her face
that I may share her elusive thoughts.
She weaves amongst the moon and stars,
warm summer skies and polar nights
before sweeping down to catch her breath
on heathered moors and mountain heights.

It was on the hills I sought her friendship,
high up on wild and craggy peaks.
Beneath clear skies I tasted bliss
and felt the kiss of her blessed presence
bonding with my needful spirit
and I knew I'd found my Paradise.

I saw her dance on moonlit stream
then glide along with silver swans.
She spread her wings over silky waters,
hovered around each woodland bole.
In silent prayer I hoped she'd linger,
keep sweet contentment within my soul.

THROUGH THE EYES OF A CHILD

Dandelion clock grasped tight in hand
she shows how she can tell the time.
Her pursed lips blow with studied try
until fine silver parachutes
float like a cloud up to the sky.

With determination, her face now rapt,
twice more yet does she huff and puff
until all downy shoots are free.
Her blue eyes twinkle as she states
'It's three o'clock Gran, did you see?'

She's sung and danced, made daisy chains
and searched for fairies in the wood.
All energy drained, her steps grow slow.
She tugs my hand to take her home
and sweetly says, 'I'm sorry Gran,
you'll have to play now on your own.'

HERON

Ankle deep on weir
he stands erect
between earth and sky,
cleric of nature's domain…
white body proud,
frock-coated in grey,
head dipped in reverence.

Neck shortened now
he preens his lower feathers,
ignores the grey stone mill behind,
belching smoke from furnace fires.
His flames are the scarlet poppies
table-clothed along the bank.
His fires are the setting sun,
the rosy blush of dawn..

He is of a different world,
mind entwined with nature;
the running of the stream,
a camouflage of reeds,
fish for his next meal.

Ignoring our satanic world
he is where he wants to be,
existing in harmony
with all living things,
lives life as it was meant to be.

THE WATER BAILIFF'S SONG

I know the river intimately,
every ripple, rivulet, pool.
I can tell you where the trout hide,
where goosanders duck and dive
to emerge way downstream
as if by some strange magic.

I see great beauty as I lay beneath
the boughs on river's bank,
watch Kingfishers dive and feed,
blue and gold arrows darting
back and forth, dizzy, busy,
under far reaching summer skies.

I can take you where the otter dines
if you'll rise before the dawn,
not startle him with chatter, only
tread with your lightest footfall.
His silver shadow sleekly diving,
a priceless pleasure of the morning.

Moving on to sunset is still proving
busy as the day now swiftly passed.
I regret that I cannot linger, no more talk,
whilst the world wends wearily to slumber.
I must go to the weir where salmon leap
where shadowy vigil I will quietly keep.

A stealthy world of quietness visits now
as cloaked in darkness comes the stranger.
Avaricious poacher, no fisherman of nature,
laying nets to skim his living's easy urge.
Maybe he is confident that he'll not meet me,
the Water Bailiff, poacher's earthly scourge.

DELUSIONS

Here I am on the checkout,
lost in this deep black hole
of toilet rolls and lettuce,
frozen peas and meat balls.
Only fluorescent lights
to guide my future
through light years,
comet flight years.

Here I am on the checkout.
They said I wasn't bright
as the moon or stars;
astrophysics, chemistry
were not for me.....
Alphabetic spaghetti more my line.
Like this frozen cod I'm battered,
mind drowning, all at sea.

Here I am on the checkout,
Bar codes invading my brain.
I am slowly going mad,
this is not the life for me.
Batman cape and mask,
Journey into Space D.V.D.
Oh fly me to the moon
Ping....ping....ping.

OUT OF THE SUN

I ran and danced and laughed and sang
down leafy lanes of endless youth,
so happy in my sun touched skin
a world of freedom, daisy chains
and childhood dreams in gilded frames.
When schooldays came I laughed with joy,
new books I treasured, read with awe.
Past deeds now told from days of old
and new lands on mapped pages drawn,
all learned with heart-felt passion borne.

I had not learned of sorrow then
nor strife, death or sad parting
and every day I'd laugh and play,
pure happiness along the way.
But the wheels of time grind onwards
to a new world where cares abide,
I have aged, grown melancholy,
those young days have now sadly died.
For in adult life I am tamed,
my spirit curbed, my laughter culled
as though my life now dulled should be
an epitome of straight laced ways
and how I miss those childhood days.

GALE

Wild winds spin the weathervane
until the cockerel looks dizzy,
North pointing South
like my life at the moment -
going in the wrong direction.

LOST HORIZON

It sits quaintly by the bend in the river,
Aunt Daisy's Boathouse Café.
Pretty gingham cloths and serviettes
and buttercups in the grass.
I was just a lass when we first met,
held hands, entranced,
like loves young dream
it might have seemed to some
but it was beautiful to hear
him say he'd always love me.

And how we laughed and danced
through that fine bluebell spring.
Carved our initials in the crooked oak
and spoke of when we two would wed.
When blue sky kissed the green
of Summer's dappled glades
we celebrated our engagement
with crumpets and Champagne
with Aunt Daisy in her café.
The sun shone as it's never shone before.

Then in Autumn's earlier days we sat
before the pungent pine wood fire,
planned our future's brightest hours,
our home, our babes and so much more.
That was before that November day
when war broke out, his 'call-up' came.
We cried and loved and tried again
to not think of all that could go wrong.
Then he was gone, my conquering hero....
words of love were lost in shell torn skies.

I sit in Aunt Daisy's Boathouse Café;
it's December again, the month I can't step past
for no future lies beyond this time.
No Christmas bells beckon and the ache of Spring
dulls the daffodils - nor can the songs
of Summer light my heart for the birdsong
sounds quite out of key or is that just me?
If I should find a darkened place to hide away
would you look down my love, think less of me?
Please show me where the sun can warm my soul.

ELEGY FOR AUTUMN

I see Autumn in it's waning days
when trees, unclothed, look quite forlorn.
Fallen leaves withered and early dawn
so bare of face, no chorus now
of pert blackbird or warbling thrush,
only the hush of deep, deep silence
and echoes of dreams forever lost.
Corn stubble fields and November mists,
unheathered moors and hedgerows bare,
the dying year is everywhere.

Is this the place that stirred my heart,
that is now stark, a cold closed door?
And I could weep for all that beauty,
the youthful days that are no more.
And would it not have been more kind
to dull my memories of this barren time
so I may live without sad dreaming,
no more that deep ache in my heart,
no more to mourn this desolation,

WHITBY 1950

Crab lines, fishing nets and maggots,
that's what the sign proclaimed
and a sea trip on 'The Blackbeard',
a pirate boat so aptly named.
And the thought of daring sea tales
in old books that I had read...
the likes of Long John Silver,
now formed pictures in my head.

Yes, we'd paddled in the shallows,
dangled lines from end pier stand
we'd fed on prawns and ice creams,
built fine castles in the sand
but my heart was with the captain
who stood by 'The Blackbeard' now
gathering the shiny shillings
to sail by the tall mast or prow.

Dressed in my sunshine yellow trunks
I sped fast over silver sand,
so careful not to miss that boat,
shilling grasped tight in small hand.
And the captain gave the children
an eye patch and a pirates hat
with skull and crossbones on the front
as down by the rigging we sat.

In my mind I sailed rough waters,
eyes searching for boats to plunder
My sharp cutlass at the ready,
and eyes so bright with wonder.
And oh the magic of those times
lives on for many a sweet year.
Filed in the folders of my mind,
those childhood memories now so dear.

SANDCASTLES -- FOUR CINQUAINS

Slowed now
the frothy flow
of silvered surf on sand
dressed in myriad seashell colours
and smiles

Our brood
build sand castles
with imagination
roused from age old books of dragons
and knights

I'm glad
the tide recedes
so the young ones won't see
their fine fortressed dreams washed away
to drown

Happy
we make for home
as stomachs ache for food
and glad hearts overflow with joy
fulfilled

FORGOTTEN

It was Autumn when he left.
No fond farewell nor message
just a world-ending empty silence.
We looked for him in the shadows,
hoped for reflections in the sunlight

but bright times had lost their form,
a final denial of past happenings.
No written word of love nor thoughts,
just an empty void that hovered.
Mum cried when the postman called.

Couldn't tell him now that
I'd come top in Maths last year,
that I'd grown so much taller,
my hair a lighter shade of brown
bleached by the summer sun…

how sad I felt when I heard
mum cry herself to sleep at night;
that we'd lost the joy of song,
each note now just an elegy
of misplaced words of love.

I wonder if he has regrets;
does he think about me, miss me?
When I marry next Easter Monday
would he be sad that it's not him,
my Dad, who's giving me away?

But it's the same old pain that twists
my feelings into a tangled knot,
forms hot tears to sting my eyes.
It's never, ever, easy to believe
that after all these years
I'm that child that he forgot.

THE COUNTRY BOY

I see briar rose kissed by soft dew,
an artist's dream of wild creation
and so I miss the bird's first song,
lost for a while in my contemplation.

But now I hear the chaffinch sing,
'You are in love with the country boy
who mends the young owl's broken wing'.

I walk quiet paths of dale and wood
and watch young fox cubs roll and play
in early morning before sunrise
when otter dives for fishy prey.

And barn owl sings his to-wit-to-woo,
'You are in love with the country boy
who brings you pearls of morning dew.'

I dangle toes in rippling stream
whilst line of thought I gently cast
and many's the hour that I look around
for my world was born in nature's past.

And I laugh with joy when thrush now calls,
'You are in love with the country boy
who re-builds the ancient limestone walls.'

Chaffinch and blackbird sing with joy
and bees now join the choral throng.
Young owl with mended wing flies in
as harebells ring a special song.

And the avian choir sings a merry lay,
'You are in love with the country boy
whom you've married on this summer's day'.

A SONG OF THE SEASONS

Cornflowers in summer, bright as my lover's eyes,
gently sway with poppies amid the golden corn.
Blackberries are ripening for nears the harvest time
and spiders spin their silver threads at dawn
as swallows soar back to a warmer clime.

Now fine the autumn's flush of golden hues
until it's beauteous cloak is gently cast aside
to set the stage for winter's scenery to follow,
when bare boughs reign and leaves lie thick
from highest hill to ragged gorse clothed hollow.

Those leaves soon lay beneath deep snow and
far moors once heathered are now bleak and white.
As winter cloaks each field and hedge
cruel north winds whip the air with spite
and icicles hang from cave and ledge.

Whilst rotted leaves now satisfy the soil
which they rekindle as they decay,
Spring soon awakes, sweet life's reborn
and bluebells cloak the woodland way
where joyous song of thrush now greets the dawn.

On clear air drifts the sweet, sweet smell
of wild rose hedge and freshly mown hay.
Spring blossom is falling like a soft May shower
around leafy bole to now prettily lay
like the dressing adorning a fine lady's bower.

The seasons pass like the strains of a song,
each with merits to rival those gone before.
Like a seed being nurtured faith is renewed
as sweet nature's roundabout turns once more,
each scene a new picture waiting to be viewed.

PARADISE REGAINED

Now our history's behind
and there's prospects ahead,
our past is old written
and our future's new born.
The clouds have diminished
here blooms a new dawn.

And the river is silver
and the river flows gentle
And the track is clear
showing us the true way.
The mist has dispersed,
sun shines on new day.

And the woods are leafy
with trees proudly blossoming
and the birds now sing
of a shining new day.
So much light from the sun
showing us the new way.

No shadows are cast for
our future's ahead,
No more pale spectres,
or worry or dread
and breeze sings with joy
as new seed has been spread.

And the mountains are tall
and the mountain air clear
and the pass overhangs
but it's nothing to fear;
our lives in our hands
and our future is clear.

And down on green flatlands
there's so much in front
and the river is silver
and the river flows fast.
Our future more certain
to now flourish and last.

FIRST LOVE

I touched the stars tonight,
flew in another time warp,
a pounding change of heartbeat
like never before.

The warm promise of your love
in gently whispered touches
sent me soaring into space,
soon floating, dreaming
at your pace.

Now in step as one
like shadows pairing;
Galactic fusion
takes my breath away.

EUTERPE
(Muse of lyric poetry and song)

It is the moon, gold, shining whole
that draws the spirits out this night,
when lyrical breath like fiery mist
swirls round the lonely, ice capped peaks.
Then Zephyrus the West wind blows,
wraps breathy arms around my form
and lifts me ever, ever skywards,
way up much closer to the moon.

And soon amongst the constellations
where asteroids and comets fly
I am the Spirit of the poem
and singer of the ancient song.
A mystery to lesser mortals
on lower lands who do not know
or understand the universe
or rhythms of the mystic winds that blow.

And when I sing amongst the stars
I feel the love of all the planets
touching me through time and space.
And I can only wonder that
although I am the smallest star
I shine with brightest heavenly light,
I am the Queen of all the night -
especially for you.

dorcas imprints